GOD'S ONLY GOSPEL

"Whosoever transgresseth, and abideth not in the doctrine of Christ, hath not God. He that abideth in the doctrine of Christ, he hath both the Father and the Son. If there come ANY unto you, and bring not THIS DOCTRINE, receiveth him not into your house, neither bid him God speed; for he that biddeth him God speed is partaker of his evil deeds." {II John 9 - 11}

Moreno Dal Bello

GOD'S ONLY GOSPEL

The Lord Jesus Christ warned that many christs would come. He said: *"**For there shall arise false christs...**"* (Matt. 24:24). He also taught that many false prophets and false teachers would come *in His very name* proclaiming that He indeed is Christ, and yet they would be deceivers who would guide many onto the broad way that leads to destruction: *"**For many shall come in My name, saying, I am Christ; and shall deceive many**"* (Matt. 24:5,11). The apostle Paul said that these deceivers would appear as *"**...ministers of righteousness...**"* yet they would in reality be ministers of Satan (2 Cor.11:13-15) who would come preaching **another gospel,** and **another jesus** and would be led by **another spirit** (2 Cor. 11:4). Paul declared that anyone, even if it were an angel come down from heaven, who would teach and thus believe any other gospel than the one he preached under the inspiration of the Holy Spirit was accursed (under the wrath of God) (Gal. 1:6-9).

      Paul did not say they were saved people who simply did not understand the doctrines of the Gospel; He said that they were in a **damned** state, (evidenced by their preaching a false gospel which showed they denied, were not submitted to and therefore not believer's in God's only Gospel), and children of wrath as are all before hearing and believing THE Gospel (Eph. 2:1-3). Paul said that *"**...if our Gospel be hid, it is hid to them that are LOST**"* (not merely in error) (2 Cor. 4:3). Also, Paul did not mean that they were reprobate—without any hope of heaven and destined for hell—he was merely saying that if one preaches and therefore believes in a false gospel they give evidence that they are, **at that point in time,** yet in an unsaved, unregenerate state. False 'christian' ministers do not come and openly deny Christ in so many words; they come in His name professing to be born again Christians. Yet in reality they are deceitful workers who transform themselves into the apostles of Christ and teach a false gospel promoting the lie that a man can by his own obedience recommend himself unto God. There is NO salvation in such a 'gospel'. **They use much truth to promote and disguise their deadly error.** Many are even very familiar with Christian terminology. Terms such as 'saved by grace' and 'mercy,' 'faith in Christ' etc., are used as part of their subtle trickery. They present themselves as something they are not. In other words outwardly and according to reputation they would indeed appear to be ministers of truth and righteousness. The apostle Paul said that grievous wolves would come and that, **"...of your own selves shall men arise, speaking perverse things, to draw away disciples after them"** (Acts 20:30). They are described by the Lord Jesus in the following warning as wolves in sheep's clothing: **"Beware of false prophets, which come to you in sheep's clothing, but inwardly they are ravening wolves"** (Matt. 7:15).

There are so many different 'gospels' today, each presenting significantly different views about the Messiah (Who He is and what He has done), that clearly the questions which should be asked by everyone who professes to be a Christian (that is, a follower of Jesus Christ) are, *"How will I know a false minister from a true one?"* and *"How can I know whether or not I have believed a false gospel or God's Gospel?"* **How is a man saved? How can we know if we are true Christians believing in the only Gospel that saves? What is God's only Gospel?** Jesus Himself asked the religious leaders of His day, **"...What think ye of Christ?..."** (Matt. 22:42). These are vital questions about which every professing believer should be concerned. With all the lies that abound in our day concerning the Gospel and true salvation the question should not be whether we *have* faith but are we in THE Faith: **"Examine yourselves, whether ye be in THE Faith..."** (2 Cor. 13:5).

THE GOSPEL IS A LIFE AND DEATH ISSUE: *"He that believeth on the Son hath everlasting life: and he that believeth not the Son shall not see life; but the wrath of God abideth on him"* (John 3:36). *"He that believeth on Him is not condemned: but he that believeth not is condemned already..."* (John 3:18).

God's Gospel is the LIFE Message! And, we must be certain that it is God's Message—HIS Gospel proclaiming HIS Christ—that we have heard and in which we have believed and trusted, and NO other. No one is saved **before** they hear this Gospel and no one is saved believing any other gospel, no matter how long they have believed it or who teaches it or endorses it. God's Gospel is about salvation by grace alone; every false gospel has one thing in common and that is they all teach a salvation by works or at least try to present a mixture of grace and works. According to Paul this is not possible: either one teaches a Gospel wholly by Grace, or one teaches that one can recommend oneself to God by obedience, **"...if by grace, then is it no more of works: otherwise grace is no more grace. But if it be of works, then is it no more grace..."** (Rom. 11:6). God will destroy all those who do not believe HIS Gospel: **"In flaming fire taking vengeance on them that know not God, and that obey not the Gospel of our Lord Jesus Christ"** (2 Thess.1:8). God is a merciful and Holy God Who by His great grace has made it abundantly clear in His Holy Word that a man can indeed know if he is a true believer or if in fact he has fallen for a false gospel wherein is no salvation. God's Gospel of Sovereign Grace is clearly presented in the Holy Scriptures.

There was only ONE Gospel given to the apostle Paul and only ONE which he ever preached and if anyone did not believe that ONE Gospel then they showed that their spiritual state was that of the damned (Gal. 1:6-9). Paul declared that it is by the Gospel that we are saved: **"...I declare unto you the Gospel...by which also ye are saved..."** (1 Cor.15:1,2). In order to be saved you have to hear this Gospel; you have to believe and trust the Gospel that comes from God, not one which comes from the imagination of man which we think sounds nice and seems right: **"There is a way which seemeth right unto a man, but the end thereof are the ways of death"** (Prov.14:12). Many preachers mention the word 'gospel' in their sermons and books but seldom do they **define** what the Gospel actually is. Some say you cannot define it. But if the Gospel cannot be defined then why would the apostle Paul have warned of another gospel. **If we cannot define, identify and distinguish what the Gospel is how then can we recognize what constitutes a false gospel?** Obviously Paul was speaking to people who knew exactly what the Gospel was because Paul had preached it to them. To recognize the false one must know the true. Others say that the Gospel is simply Jesus Christ; we must go further than this and ask ourselves: **Yes, but Who is Jesus Christ and what did He do and for whom did He do it?** We must distinguish the True Christ from the counterfeits. The Christ Whom Paul spoke about is not the christ which the false teachers of his day were promoting. Otherwise he would never have warned of another jesus. Paul's Christ is ONE specific individual and unique Person distinct from all others who accomplished something specific. Paul did not offer assurance to those who merely call on the name of some historical figure known as 'Jesus'. Most people know that Jesus died on a cross and was resurrected three days later, even the demons know this and tremble, but this is not saving knowledge for if it was then most would be saved including Satan and his angels. **Knowing Christ savingly is knowing Who He is and what He has done and for whom He has done it not simply what happened to Him.** One can know ABOUT a person but that does not necessarily mean that one actually KNOWS that person. The Bible teaches that **"...Christ died for our sins according to the Scriptures"**(1 Cor.15:3). The True Christ did exactly what the Scriptures foretold He would do. THIS is the Christ in Whom we are to believe: **the One of Whom Scripture speaks.** Christ died according to the Scriptures. Jesus fulfilled what was prophesied about Him: how He died, why He had to die, what He would accomplish by His death, for whom He died, and so forth, according to the Scriptures. Thus, the details of Christ's life, death and resurrection are vital if we are to recognize and believe the True Gospel, for they speak of Him—Who He is and what He has done and for whom He has done it. They identify Him as the True Christ and set Him apart from the counterfeits. **One cannot separate Who Christ is from what Christ has done. One cannot have the True Christ if one does not believe in**

what the True Christ did. Some protest and say, *"Not all are theologians. You don't have to know doctrine; you just have to know HIM."* One man's response to this absurd and dangerous reasoning is, *"The only way you CAN know HIM is by the Gospel doctrine, the doctrine of Christ, that identifies and distinguishes HIM from counterfeits"* (WP). **People say its not important WHAT you believe but WHOM you believe. But surely WHAT you believe about whom you believe DEFINES the one you believe!** The True Christ is revealed in the Bible which is the Word (doctrine, ie., teachings) of God. The Bible asks: *"How then shall they call on Him in Whom they have not believed? and how shall they believe in Him of Whom they have not heard? and how shall they hear without a preacher? And how shall they preach, except they be sent?..."* (Rom. 10:14, 15). One cannot and never has called on the True Jesus if one has not believed on the True Jesus; One cannot and never has believed on Him if one has not heard of Him: Who He is and what He has done and for whom He has done it; and, one cannot and never has heard of Him: Who He is and what He has done, if one has not had HIM preached by a preacher sent of God or read about Him in Scripture. Jesus said: *"And this is life eternal, that they might KNOW Thee the ONLY true God, and Jesus Christ, Whom Thou hast sent"* (John 17:3; see also Jer. 9:23,24; Phil. 3:10). **Salvation itself is incompatible with ignorance of Who Christ is and what Christ has done.**

It is clear that we cannot distinguish the false preachers of a false gospel from the true by observing their outward acts of righteousness, by their morality, by their expressed love for Jesus, by their perceived sincerity or passion for the 'gospel' they preach, by their reputation among men, by who endorses them, by how many books they have written or how many sermons they have preached or how wide their smile is when saying Christ's name (Matt. 23:27,28). A true preacher of the Gospel **can** be distinguished from the false preacher by judging whether or not he preaches the Gospel of Jesus Christ—**by examining the doctrines he teaches.** Does he preach the True Christ or another jesus? One has wisely stated that **"it is a man's**

doctrine which identifies and distinguishes the God he worships and serves" (WP). All false religion is based upon a false knowledge of who God is and what He has done. If one were to say to you that they know your father but then gave a wrong description of him and attributed to him things that you know your father has never done, or not attributed to him things which you know he did do, it would not only show that they were in error but that they in fact **DID NOT KNOW** your father AT ALL! They may have heard of him but they do not KNOW him.

The Lord Jesus warned His followers to beware of false prophets (teachers). Therefore it is obvious that if it is necessary that true believers are to be on their guard against false prophets, and their false gospels, then it **must** be possible to distinguish the true from the false if we are to flatly reject the false and embrace the true (1 Cor. 2:15). Not only is it possible to discern between the true and the false but it is incumbent upon every believer to do so. The Lord Jesus warned His disciples: **"...Take heed and beware of the leaven of the Pharisees and of the Sadducees"** (Matt. 16:6). He later explained that the leaven about which He spoke was in fact the **doctrine** of the Pharisees and Sadducees (Matt. 16:12). In other words, Jesus warned of false teachings. Those who come in Christ's name and who preach false doctrines concerning Christ and His Gospel always have some truth mixed in with their lies. But when one mixes error with truth one always ends up with a lie. No matter how much good food is mixed in with poison the substance will still be labelled **POISONOUS!!** A little error added to a big truth makes the whole thing one big error, one big lie, (eg. $2 + 2 = 4$) **"A little leaven leaveneth the whole lump"** (Gal. 5:9). The Word of God is to be the Standard, the Measure by which we can always judge the false from the true. After hearing the preaching of Paul the Bereans **"...searched the Scriptures daily, whether those things were so"** (Acts 17:11). The true believer is not to judge according to appearance or reputation, **either in a negative sense or even in a positive sense,** for all is not always what it appears to be, but he must judge righteous judgement; he must judge according to the Word of God, according to what GOD has said. Christ Jesus commanded that we **"Judge not according to the appearance, but judge righteous judgement"** (John 7:24). Paul added **"But he that is spiritual judgeth all things..."** (1 Cor.2:15). **It is a man's MESSAGE on which we should concentrate, not his personality, outward show of morality and uprightness, or his reputation.** Paul illustrated this by teaching that even if he or an angel from heaven were to come down and teach another gospel, other than the one which Paul HAD preached, he should not be listened to simply because it was Paul or an angel speaking, but his message should be analysed, and if it is not God's Message then he should be shunned and avoided (Gal. 1:8,9; Rom. 16:17,18; Acts 17:11). Paul was so sure that what he preached was The Eternal Gospel of Jesus Christ that he told his hearers that if he ever returned to them telling of a different gospel they were not to believe him! The apostle John states: **"Beloved, believe not every spirit, but try the spirits whether they are of God: because many false prophets are gone out into the world"** (1 John 4:1; see also 1 Thess. 5:21). No one in their right mind would judge a suspect meal to be free of poison simply by its outward appearance and then proceed to eat it but by carefully and correctly analysing the contents. Most people today are swayed into believing the message before they even hear it simply because it is a certain messenger who is speaking or because of the denomination to which he belongs, or because *"he's been the pastor at our church for 30 years".* Just because a man has been preaching the same message for 30 years is no guarantee that his message is God's Message.

      The Bible teaches that in order for a man to believe the true Gospel He must be blessed of God; he must be born again—born of God (Matt. 16:17; John 3:3,5; 6:44,45), for the Gospel is God's and He reveals It to whomsoever He wills. Salvation is not and never has been as the result or product of a man's will or works but wholly of God's mercy and grace: **"...I will have mercy on whom I will have mercy, and I will have compassion on whom I will have compassion. So then it is not of him that willeth, nor of him that** *runneth, but OF GOD that sheweth mercy"* (Rom. 9:15,16; Ex. 33:19). Speaking of those who believe on Christ's name, John the apostle stated: *"Which were born, not of blood, nor of the will of the flesh, nor of the will of man, but OF GOD"* (John 1:13; see also 1 Cor.1:29-31). The faith that saves is not something which originates from within man, it is not a work that he can produce by nature, but it is in fact a precious gift from God, it is something which has to be given to a man not something which can be earned *"For by GRACE are ye saved through faith; and that NOT OF YOURSELVES: it is the GIFT OF GOD: NOT OF WORKS, lest any man should boast"* (Eph. 2:8, 9). It is the faith **of** Jesus Christ, that which comes from Him, that is, finds its origin in Him and not in us, which truly leads a person to believe in Him (Phil. 3:9). The faith that comes from man that spawns his best religious efforts and sincerest moral reformations can only lead to a false christ—an idol—a false religion, and to ultimate destruction, for man is corrupted, and his heart is deceitful above all things and desperately wicked (Jer.17:9) so that all of man's judgements are based on a darkened understanding. *"He that trusteth in his own heart is a fool..."* (Prov. 28:26). *"Who can bring a clean thing out of an unclean? not one"* (Job 14:4).

According to Scripture salvation is not something which is or can be gained or achieved by any effort on man's part—not even by believing (by one's faith); **salvation is not a reward** for our work of belief (Rom. 4:4,5), but is something that is given to a man purely by the grace (**unmerited** favor) of God. **FAITH IS NOT A CONDITION FOR SALVATION—IT IS AN EVIDENCE OF SALVATION.** The first evidence, or result, of salvation is saving faith, which is a **Gift of God**; originates with Him. This is the faith—the ONLY faith—that can and does savingly believe God's one and only Gospel, and that eternally, for it is of God, and it is His to give. Jesus said: *"It is the Spirit that quickeneth;* (makes alive) *the flesh profiteth nothing...therefore said I unto you, that no man CAN come unto Me, except it were GIVEN unto him of My Father"* (John 6:63,65). Coming to God in the acceptable way is a result of His grace upon the sinner and not the outcome of a man's efforts.

Coming to God according to man's ways and thoughts leads only to death (Num. 3:4).

The faith that comes as a gift from God causes the elect of God to **forever** believe and abide in the Gospel—the doctrine of Jesus Christ—the terms of which are vital to a saving knowledge of Him: **Who He is and what He has done and for whom He has done it.** Firstly, in order to understand what the Gospel is all about and why it is so necessary, we need to set ourselves the proper biblical foundation. To do so, we must consider the Fall of mankind. The true recipient of God's mercy will believe that the Fall of man caused by the sin of Adam in the Garden of Eden brought about the spiritual death not only of Adam and Eve but also their seed: the entire race of man which came out of them and who were represented in Adam (Gen. 2:16,17; 3:1-7). **"...as by the offence of one judgement came upon all men to condemnation..."** (Rom. 5:18). **"...by one man's disobedience many were made sinners..."** (Rom. 5:19). **"Wherefore, as by one man sin entered into the world, and death by sin; and so death passed upon all men, for that all have sinned"** (Rom. 5:12). This first sin of disobedience, or unbelief, committed by man separated him from God for all eternity. Do and live, disobey and die was the law God had set for man. God said to Adam, **"But of the tree of the knowledge of good and evil, thou shalt not eat of it: for in the day that thou eatest thereof thou shalt surely die"** (Gen. 2:17). It introduced corruption into the race of man. It introduced sickness and physical, as well as spiritual death, the corruption of the flesh and soul of man. It made man into an unholy and unclean thing. However, it did not make him into a creature that would utterly despise the notion of the existence of a Supreme Being, although in some cases this would be so; but for the majority, the sense or desire to worship, though severely perverted, would not be lost. It would mean that they (the world) would insist on seeking God in their own way, according to their terms rather than God's terms. They would not, indeed they could not, come to Him His Way, for they were dead to Him, to His ways and His Thoughts, and alive to sin and the desire to please themselves and to do what was right in their own eyes. Man became a self-righteous creature without the Life and Light of God. Man's heart became evil, **"The heart is deceitful above all things, and desperately wicked..."** (Jer. 17:9). **"...the heart of the sons of men is full of evil, and madness is in their heart while they live..."** (Eccl. 9:3; see also Eccl. 7:29; Jer. 2:21).

The first thing Adam and Eve did after they'd sinned was to attempt to cover up the shame of their sin. They clothed themselves with fig leaves to hide their shame yet they hid themselves from God. They had clothed themselves because of the guilt and shame of sin and hid themselves for fear of punishment (Gen. 3:10). This is precisely what every man does in his natural sinful state. He tries to 'get right with God' by feebly trying to cover up his sin or thinking that he can make up for it by obeying the law and becoming moral; by reforming his life and becoming obedient, keeping the Ten Commandments etc., **but a morality without Christ is death!** This would be like a rotten apple trying to emit a pleasant aroma in an attempt to do away with its rottenness. The Lord Jesus puts it this way: **"...neither can a corrupt tree bring forth good fruit"** (Matt. 7:18). Man's best efforts, as we shall see, at trying to please a Holy God fall far short of what God's Holiness demands. Through His mercy, **it was God who came to man** and called out to him and later clothed him and taught him how He was to be approached and worshipped in the acceptable way (Gen. 3:8-24).

Romans 3 clearly shows man's fallen and destitute condition. **"As it is written, there is none righteous, no, not one"** (Rom. 3:10). The Bible does not say that there are none moral or zealously religious, but that there are none who are in right standing with God, **"For all have sinned, and come short of the glory of God"** (Rom. 3:23). All are sinners and unclean without a righteousness that meets the demands of God's Holy Law. All fall short of perfection which God's Holy Law demands from man. In fact, Scripture says that **"... verily every man at his best state is altogether vanity"** (Psa. 39:5). **"And all the inhabitants of the earth are reputed as nothing..."** (Dan. 4:35). **"For there is not a just man upon earth, that doeth good, and sinneth not"** (Eccl. 7:20). **"There is none that understandeth..."**

(Rom. 3:11). This shows that no man in his natural fallen state has any true perception of God and His way of Salvation; instead, he only has a rebellious rejection stemming from a perverted view of God. Natural man cannot understand the things of God, for these things can only be spiritually discerned by those whom He has made alive unto Him: **"But the natural man receiveth not the things of the Spirit of God: for they are foolishness unto him: neither can he know them, because they are spiritually discerned"** (see 1Cor.2:9-14). **"...there is none that seeketh after God"** (Rom. 3:11), that is, seeks after Him His Way. **"They are all gone out of the way..."** (Rom. 3:12) the only way of salvation that honors the Redemptive Character of God and excludes all occasions of boasting in the sinner. To summarize, **"There is no fear of God before their eyes"** (Rom. 3:18).

Contrary to what most people believe, every man by nature is not a child of God but a child of wrath (Eph. 2:3), and a child of the Devil (Matt.13:38; Jn. 8:44) man drinks iniquity like water (Job 15:15,16) and is depraved in mind (Eph 4:17-19). He is a creature whose mind has been blinded (2 Cor. 4:3,4), who cannot hear the words of Christ (Jn. 8:33,34) and therefore cannot know the things of God (1 Cor. 2:14). This is the result of Original Sin. Man in his natural state cannot ever please God (Rom. 8:8), for without the Faith **of** God no man can please Him (Heb. 11:6). As one man has wisely stated, man does not have any earning power with God, because man is a sinner. Man cannot produce any good work that is pleasing to a Perfect and Just God, for God demands perfect Righteousness which no man can produce. Man has no redeeming quality. Even the apostle Paul said: **For I know that in me (that is, in my flesh,) dwelleth no good thing..."** (Rom. 7:18). No man is ever going to become right with God by any work that he does or abstains from doing, for man is a sinner, and everything he does is stained with sin (Rom. 3:20). The Bible states that man sits in spiritual darkness and is enslaved to Satan and in bondage to sin (Luke 1:79; 2 Tim. 2:26; John 8:34). He is without God and therefore without hope in this world (Eph. 2:12), and can never do anything to change his condition—who he is and what he is: **"Can the Ethiopian change his skin, or the leopard his spots? then may ye also do good, that are accustomed to do evil"** (Jer. 13:23). Man's condition, or nature, is that of a hater of God's Truth and a lover of Satan's lie (2 Thess. 2:10-12). Jesus Christ the Lord states: **"And this is the condemnation, that light is come into the world, and men loved darkness rather than light, because their deeds were evil. For everyone that doeth evil hateth the light, neither cometh to the light..."** (John 3:19, 20; 5:40). The evil deeds of natural sinful man are not merely his immoral actions and thoughts but include his best efforts at religion in order to make himself acceptable to God. There are many religious, many who even call Jesus Christ "Lord", yet they will never see Heaven (Matt. 7:21).

If one **refuses** to believe the above statements in reference to the hopelessly sinful state of every man and woman to come out of Adam's seed, and in particular the Scriptures cited concerning the condition of man in Adam after the Fall, then there is no way they will ever believe the true Gospel of God. Every teaching, even if it is an angel from heaven teaching it, that does not clearly declare that man is DEAD in sin and cannot and therefore will not come to God **God's Way** will lead a man to believe in a false gospel which proclaims that salvation is conditioned on man. **Those who reject the doctrine that man by nature is dead in sin and cannot in and of himself desire to or do anything to come to God God's Way believe that salvation is conditioned on the sinner and clearly deny salvation by grace alone.** All false gospels leave room for a man to boast in his salvation by teaching that man is not completely dead to God but can indeed choose Him of his own free will. This is an old heresy known as *Pelagianism*. The modern version is called *Arminianism*—a refuge, as one man has observed, for modern blinded patrons of human self-sufficiency. *"God has done His part"* (they say), *"and now it is up to us to choose Him. God has no say in the matter; He cannot and will not interfere in man's decision-making for He is a gentleman."*

This false teaching leads one to believe in the lie that man in his natural state is not a lover of spiritual darkness or a servant of sin, that he is not in bondage to it, but that he can freely abandon sin where and when he chooses, and that his will is not a slave to sin but is just as free as it was before the Fall or is at least made that way for a time by something they call *'prevenient grace'*. Christ Jesus states quite clearly: **"Verily, verily, I say unto you, whosoever committeth sin is the servant of sin"** (John 8:34).

God warned Adam that in the day he ate of the forbidden fruit he would die (Gen. 2:17). Satan countered by telling Eve that she would *not* die (Gen. 3:4). Which do you believe: God's truth or Satan's lie? Those who believe Satan say that man is not totally depraved or totally incapable of coming to God God's way but that man is merely partially depraved, he is not spiritually dead but merely sin-sick. Wounded by the Fall but not mortally. Man is not drowned in sin but is simply drown-*ing* and awaits a lifesaver to be thrown to him which he would immediately take hold of. Satan's lie, his speaking words of peace to Eve, is promoted and believed in by most who profess to be Christians. The word 'die' as used by God in His warning to Adam means 'dead', 'worthy of death,' 'destroy,' 'die,' 'kill,' 'slay very suddenly'. In fact, in EVERY instance where the word 'die' is used in both Old and New Testaments **ALL** speak of death, **NONE** refer to merely a state of sickness! Ephesians 2:1 speaks of man being **dead** in trespasses and sins. And in verse 5 of the same chapter it speaks of Jesus making ALIVE (not well) those who were DEAD (not sick). Along with many other scriptures Colossians 2:13 also speaks of sinners being dead in their sins. When the Lord Jesus said that a man must be born again if he is to see the Kingdom of God (John 3:3), He could not have meant that a man must be physically re-born for man has been given but one life to live (Heb. 9:27). Jesus was speaking of a man being **spiritually** born again, to be spiritually regenerated. To be brought back to spiritual life from a state of spiritual death. **All who believe man is merely sin-sick believe and promote Satan's lie to Eve that she would not surely die for they say "we are not surely dead".**

It, therefore, stands to biblical reason that if man is dead in sin and cannot in and of himself come

to God, then we are left with only one alternative: it is God that must come to man if any man is to be saved. Scripture says that: *"...salvation is of the Lord"* (Jon. 2:9). Indeed, the Scriptures speak of the Lord Jesus as *"...the Captain of their salvation..."* (Heb. 2:10). To attribute any part of salvation to man is blasphemy against God. Jesus Christ insists that: *"No man CAN come to Me, except the Father which hath sent Me draw him..."* (John 6:44; see also Matt. 11:27). This *drawing* is done by their being taught of God: *"...every man therefore that hath heard, and hath LEARNED of the Father, cometh unto Me"* (John 6:45). **Jesus Himself said that with man salvation is impossible but with God all things are possible—yes—even the salvation of a man!** (Mark 10:26,27; Jer. 32:17).

If it is not man who chooses God, then it must be God Who chooses man. Since it is patently obvious that not all have believed, we must conclude that not all are chosen (Matt. 20:16). God has chosen to save some in His great mercy motivated by his Sovereign Purpose and Grace and His Covenant Love (2 Tim.1:9). This is exactly what He has done from BEFORE the foundation of the world, showing clearly that election was not based on anything man had done for man did not yet exist! *"...He hath chosen us in Him BEFORE the foundation of the world..."* (Eph. 1:4; 2 Thess. 2:13). God did not choose man according to any man's works, actual or foreseen for every man sits in spiritual darkness and all his attempts at pleasing God are evil until God comes to him. Nothing in man's character and conduct appealed to or impressed the Holy God in any way. *"But God commendeth His love toward us, in that, WHILE WE WERE YET SINNERS, Christ died for us"* (Rom. 5:8). God has not chosen all people but **A** people, a remnant, out of every nation to become His people and for Him to be their God (Rev. 5:9). The elect of God are a chosen generation not a generation of choosers: *"But ye are a chosen generation...a peculiar people; that ye should shew forth the praises of Him who hath called you out of darkness into His marvellous light"* (1 Pet. 2:9). God elected man before the world was even created, so how, we may ask, could election ever be based on what man would or could do? (see Eph 1:4,5,11; Acts 13:48; Rom. 8:29,30; 9:11-13, 18-21; Psa. 65:4; 1 Thess. 5:9; 2 Thess. 2:13). God did not choose any because He foresaw that they would love and choose Him for: **"We love Him, BECAUSE HE FIRST loved us"** (1 John 4:19).

God's election of a man to eternal life is not conditioned on anything that man does or abstains from doing: **"Not by works of righteousness which we have done, but according to His mercy He saved us..."** (Titus 3:5).This is good news because if salvation were conditioned on man then none would be saved for no man could ever meet any condition perfectly which is what a Holy God demands. It is purely an election by grace, **"And if by grace, then is it no more of works: otherwise grace is no more grace..."** (Rom. 11:6; see also Gal. 2:21). You cannot merge grace and works for the one cancels out the other. The apostle Paul stated **"I do not frustrate the grace of God: for if righteousness come by the law, then Christ is dead in vain"** (Gal. 2:21). Paul is saying that if salvation is by our obedience to God's law then salvation is not by grace and Christ Jesus simply wasted His time and efforts **for salvation is not by grace if we can attain it by our works: "Now to him that worketh is the reward not reckoned of grace, but of debt"** (Rom. 4:4). God **"...hath saved us, and called us with an holy calling, not according to our works, but according to His own purpose and grace, which was given us in Christ Jesus before the world began"** (2 Tim.1:9). **"But we believe that through the grace of the Lord Jesus Christ we shall be saved..."** (Acts 15:11). **"For we through the Spirit wait for the hope of righteousness BY FAITH"** (not by works) (Gal. 5:5). *"The very concept of grace is salvation conditioned on Christ"* (WP). Salvation is unmeritable. Man cannot do anything to earn grace or mercy for then they would cease to be grace and mercy. **Salvation is something man can never attain for it is not something which can be attained only received;** it is not a reward but a Gift. Salvation cannot be earned therefore it must be received as a gift. Man can never earn or merit salvation as he has earned and fully merits his destruction, **"For the wages of sin is**

death; but the GIFT of God is eternal life through Jesus Christ our Lord" (Rom. 6:23)."*When salvation and blessings are said to be of grace it means that the recipient has met NO conditions to earn it or appropriate it and that he has no claim upon it by way of* (personal) *merit*" (WP). It is therefore UNMERITED favor which God has for His elect children. The Bible says that: ***"...by the deeds of the law there shall no flesh be justified in His sight..."*** (Rom. 3:20)—the sight of a Holy God—***"...no man is justified by the law in the sight of God..."*** (Gal. 3:11). If salvation could be attained by obedience to the Law of God then Christ would not have been required to save any for man would be his own savior. Paul the apostle states that ***"...if righteousness come by the law, then Christ is dead in vain"*** (Gal. 2:21). Man would have to obey God's Law perfectly; he would have to be perfect himself, to have never sinned, to be in right standing with God: ***"Cursed is everyone that continueth not in ALL things which are written in the book of the law to do them"*** (Gal. 3:10). In fact, man would have to be God because no mere man could "*produce an everlasting righteousness of infinite value to be applied to a multitude of sinners. Only God could provide a righteousness of infinite value to save the whole election of grace*" (WP). But Scripture makes it plain that ***"...by the obedience of ONE shall many be made Righteous*** (Rom. 5:19). *As Creator, Ruler and Judge, God is at liberty to deal with a world of sinners according to His own good pleasure. He can rightly pardon some and condemn others; can rightfully give His saving grace to one and not to another. Since all have sinned and come short of His glory, He is free to have mercy on whom He will have mercy* (Rom. 9:16). The potter may do what he wills with the clay—how much more God who MADE the clay! ***"...cannot I do with you as this potter? saith the Lord. Behold, as the clay is in the potter's hand, so are ye in Mine hand..."*** (Jer. 18:6; Rom. 9:21). It is the love and grace and mercy of God that we are to be taken up with in amazement that He has chosen to save any. In answer to Moses asking Him to show him His Glory, God answered: ***"...I will make all My GOODNESS pass before thee, and I will proclaim the***

name of the Lord before thee; and will be gracious to whom I will be gracious, and will shew mercy on whom I will shew mercy" (Ex. 33:19). Man is deserving of death, hell and eternal punishment and God was not obligated to save any, but graciously He has predestinated unto salvation a remnant out of every nation *"...being predestinated according to the purpose of Him who worketh all things after the counsel of His own will"* (not yours) (Eph. 1:11). Those who will not believe God's Gospel shall rightly and justly be damned for eternity: *"That they all might be damned WHO BELIEVED NOT THE TRUTH, but had pleasure in unrighteousness"* (2 Thess. 2:12; Psa. 78:22). Paul said those that perish do so because *"...they received not the love of the truth, that they might be saved"* (2 Thess. 2:10).

But wait! Surely it is not enough for God to simply choose a people in order that they might be saved and escape the punishment of hell for all eternity, for God is a Holy and Just God **whose Law demands to be fulfilled and whose inflexible Justice demands to be satisfied** for any to enter heaven. It is God Himself Who has said that no sinner will escape punishment, He *"...will by no means clear the guilty..."* (Ex. 34:7), for *"...the soul that sinneth, it shall die"* (Ezek. 18:4). **Payment for sin must be made, and a perfect obedience established, or the sinner must go to his place of destruction.** As man cannot pay the price of his sins, an atonement—an appeasement—must therefore be made on the behalf of man for all his sins in order that he might be made free from the guilt and punishment he has earned as a reward for his sinfulness. A sacrifice must be performed for *"...without shedding of blood is no remission"* (Heb. 9:22; see also Lev. 17:11). But man cannot atone for his own sin; he cannot pay the price that is due his sin. He cannot in any way, shape or form make up for (or even begin to make up for) what he has done, let alone for anybody else for man is an unclean creature polluted by sin. He virtually reeks of it. Man can never make up for his sin, for in everything he does, he sins again. The Bible states clearly that man's very righteousness is as filthy rags to a Holy God, *"But we are all as an unclean thing, and all* *our righteousnesses are as filthy rags..."* (Isa. 64:6); *"Behold, He putteth no trust in His saints; yea, the heavens are not clean in His sight. How much more abominable and filthy is man, which drinketh iniquity like water?"* (Job 15:15,16). What an unregenerate religious man who holds to a false gospel and who is convinced he is a Christian, calls *'wonderful works,'* Jesus the Lord calls **'iniquity'** (Matt. 7:22,23). If man's best works, his best efforts at religion, cannot make him acceptable to a Holy God or even contribute in the smallest way to his salvation, then this atonement, this satisfaction of God's justice, this blotting out of man's sin, must come from another. But there is no man ever born that could do this for every one born of the seed of man carries within him the seed of sin.

However, all is not lost. As the Holy Scriptures often say: **"But God!!!!"** God in the richness of His mercy and in the love wherewith He loved His chosen ones came to this earth as a Man Himself to live as a man, as a Substitute for His people, the perfect sinless life that none of us could ever live, in order that He might establish the perfect Righteousness of which man was in desperate need but could never produce: *"...by the obedience of ONE shall many be made Righteous* (Rom. 5:19); Jesus Christ, the Second Person of the Blessed Trinity, came to this earth approximately 2,000 years ago, born of a virgin, **not of the seed of man but of the Seed of God.** By means of the Holy Spirit of God, Jesus was conceived in the virgin Mary's womb, free of any stain of sin, and He lived a perfect life in obedience to God and His Holy Law: *"But when the fullness of the time was come, God sent forth His Son, made of a woman, made under the law, to redeem them that were under the law, that we might receive the adoption of sons"* (Gal. 4:4,5). **Christ did not come to redeem good people who had met certain conditions, but ungodly sinners who could not meet any of the demands of God's holy law:** *"For when we were yet without strength, in due time Christ died for the UNGODLY"* (Rom 5:6-10; 4:5). Everything Jesus did was pleasing to God (Matt. 3:17). Every thought, word, and deed were all perfect, and He remained obedient throughout His life on earth even to dying on a cross to atone for the sins of all those whom God had given Him. Jesus Christ was the Atonement that God's chosen ones required in order to have their sins abolished and blotted out: **"For Christ also hath once suffered for sins, the Just for the unjust, that He might bring us to God..."** (1 Pet. 3:18). The sins of God's sheep were **imputed,** or **legally charged** to, Christ's account and nailed to the cross: **"Christ hath redeemed US from the curse of the law, being made a curse for us..."** Gal. 3:13).**"Blotting out the handwriting of ordinances that was against us, which was contrary to us, and took it out of the way, nailing it to His cross"** (Col. 2:14). In this way, by way of IMPUTATION, God could and would remain Just AND be the Justifier of all those whom He had chosen to believe on His Son (Rom. 3:25-28; see also Rom. 8:29-31). Christ Jesus was the Propitiation, or Satisfaction for all their sins (1 John 2:2). God's Holy Justice was satisfied in Christ's death for the sins of man for He was a Perfect Offering to God made on the behalf of all God's chosen ones (Heb. 9:26-28; see also Eph. 5:2). He was and is their Savior, their Substitute, their Advocate, their High Priest; their Redeemer, their Mediator, their Surety, their Representative. Just as Adam represented the whole human race in the Garden of Eden, so, too, in His obedience and in His death on Calvary's Hill, Jesus Christ represented all those whom the Father had given Him: **"For if by one man's offence death reigned by one; much more they which receive abundance of grace and of the GIFT OF RIGHTEOUSNESS shall reign in life by ONE, Jesus Christ"** (Rom. 5:17; see also John 6:37; 17:2; Heb. 2:13). God the Father has laid on God the Son all the sins of all His elect: **"...the Lord hath laid on Him the iniquity of us all"** (Isa. 53:6). Christ offered Himself to bear (carry away) the sins of His sheep: **"So Christ was once offered to bare the sins of many..."** (Heb. 9:28; see also Titus 2:14). **"And ye know that He was manifested to take away our sins..."** (1 John 3:5; see also Matt. 1:21; Luke 1:77). All the sins of all His people have been washed away in His own blood and are now removed as far as east is from the west (Psa. 103:12). **"...Unto Him that loved US, and washed US** *from **OUR** sins in His own blood"* (Rev. 1:5). The penalty for the sins of all His people has been paid IN FULL FOR ALL TIME *"...we are sanctified through the offering of the Body of Jesus Christ once for all"* (Heb. 10:10; Col. 2:13). Christ Jesus the Lord, who is the Good Shepherd, said: *"I am the good shepherd: the good shepherd giveth His life for the sheep"* and *"...I lay down My life for the sheep"* (John 10:11,15). Christ so loved the Church that He gave Himself exclusively for it: *"Husbands, love your wives, even as Christ also loved the Church, and gave Himself for it"* (Eph. 5:25); *"Who gave Himself for **US**, that He might redeem **US** from **ALL** iniquity, and purify unto Himself a peculiar* (special, one's own) *people, zealous of good works"* (Titus 2:14). In illustrating the love of God for His people the apostle John, writing to Christians, said: *"...He laid down His life for **US**..."* (1 John 3:16). And Paul the apostle speaking to Christians, said: *"Christ hath redeemed **US** from the curse of the law, being made a curse for us..."* (Gal. 3:13). Scripture says that Christ *"...took on Him the seed of Abraham"* and was *"made like unto His brethren"* (Heb. 2:16,17). Who is the seed of Abraham? *"And if ye be Christ's, then are ye Abraham's seed, and heirs according to the promise"* (Gal. 3:29; see also Rom. 4:16). These are the ones whom Christ Jesus came to save. Where there is remission of sins there is no future offering required or condition to be met in order to justify the sinner: *"Now where remission of these* (sins and iniquities) *is, there is no more offering for sin"* (Heb. 10:18). It is Christ's death, the shedding of His blood, on the behalf of the sinner and not any condition which the sinner has to meet which ratifies the New Covenant: *"...for this cause He is the Mediator of the new testament, that by means of death...they which are called might receive the promise of eternal inheritance"* (Heb. 9:15-17). The called of God are a special people, God's own people, who will not experience the wrath of God for the Lord Jesus laid down His life for them: *"For God hath not appointed **US** to wrath, but to obtain salvation by our Lord Jesus Christ, Who died for **US**..."* (1 Thess. 5:9,10). The elect have an appointment with salvation made by God Himself!

Now with all the sins of all God's chosen, His Church, paid for by the very Son of God Himself, man needed one more thing to make him totally acceptable to God, and that was to be as Righteous—as Perfect—as He is, for the Holy God of the Universe accepts nothing that is not of Him. We who are unjust must be made Just; we who are unrighteous must be made Righteous and we who are unholy must be made holy in order that we may dwell in the Presence of the Holy One. This, too, was done by the sinless Son, Jesus Christ, Who not only took on Him the sins of His people but His very own Righteousness was imputed—or charged to their account—so that legally, or positionally, all God's elect could be presented to Him free of the stain of sin **and** with the Perfect Righteousness which God's Law demands. This is summed up in 2 Corinthians 5:21: **"For He hath made Him to be sin for us, Who knew no sin; that we might be made the Righteousness of God in Him."** As our Great High Priest (Heb. 4:14) Jesus the Lord offered up His own blood on the behalf of His own people to atone for or make a covering for their sins, just as the Old Testament high priest who was merely a shadow or a type of the TRUE High Priest Who was to come, offered up the blood of animals, not for the whole world, but for a particular people—the nation of Israel (Heb. 9:7-16). **The Atonement in Scripture was always something which was definite for the persons intended and represented by the high priest.** David rejoiced and counted blessed those **"...unto whom God imputeth righteousness WITHOUT WORKS"** (Rom. 4:6), that is, without having met any prior condition to merit that Holy Righteousness. David also said: **"Blessed is he whose transgression is forgiven, whose sin is covered. Blessed is the man unto whom the Lord imputeth not iniquity..."** (Psa.32:1,2; see also 2 Cor. 5:19). The Gospel is the Good News of Salvation conditioned on the atoning Blood and Imputed Righteousness of Christ alone.

One can only trust in the true Christ Who has done such wonders **after** one has heard and believed the true Gospel which is the only one which speaks of that Christ, **"In whom ye also trusted, AFTER that ye heard the Word of Truth, THE Gospel of your salvation..."** (Eph. 1:11-14;

see also Col. 1:5,6). **One cannot trust in the True Christ after having heard a false gospel!** No one has ever been saved by hearing a false preacher led by a false spirit proclaiming a false gospel which tells of a false christ. A false gospel can do nothing but declare and promote a false christ otherwise Paul the apostle would never have called a man who brings a false gospel 'accursed' (Gal.1:8,9). **No one is blessed who is accursed, and no one who calls a man blessed whom the Holy Spirit calls accursed can themselves be in a blessed state, or saved.** (See Galatians 1:8,9). **Whoever heard of a man preaching a false gospel and a true Christ, or the true Gospel but a false christ, at the same time!** And whoever heard of a saved man preaching a false gospel? False preachers are counterfeits who preach a counterfeit gospel which tells of a counterfeit christ who can only offer a counterfeit salvation! God's ministers proclaim HIS Gospel and HIS Christ and no other. The two are inextricably connected. This shows clearly that God's only Gospel speaks of Who Christ is and what Christ has done and for whom He has done it. One cannot come to the True Christ unless God reveals to you doctrinal truth (His Gospel) which identifies both His person AND His Work and gives you the faith to believe in His Christ. **It is God's only Gospel which identifies and distinguishes God's only Jesus from all counterfeits.** No one can come to Him unless they have first LEARNED of Him from the Father (John 6:44,45). **The Christ that saves must be properly and clearly identified and distinguished, and His work clearly defined in order that He can be set apart from all counterfeits before He can be believed in.** If one believes and teaches a false gospel and false christ then it is of a certainty that that man has NOT been taught by the Holy Spirit of God. The Holy Spirit is the Spirit of Truth and will never lead a man to believe a false gospel or another Christ (John 14:17; 15:26; 16:13), **"For as many as are led by the Spirit of God, they are the sons of God"** (Rom. 8:14). The Lord Jesus says: **"...every man therefore that hath heard, and hath learned of the Father, cometh unto Me"** (John 6:45).

The first evidence of spiritual life, of being born again, is belief of this Gospel and ONLY this Gospel. The true believer will also believe in light of the above that he in and of himself could never have done anything to come to God in the proper and acceptable way. He will believe that Christ's Blood and Righteousness ensured and demanded his salvation. Man needs God. Remember Jesus' words, **'with man salvation is impossible...'** It is Christ that makes a man acceptable: **To the praise of the glory of His grace, wherein HE HATH MADE US ACCEPTED in the Beloved"** (Eph. 1:6,7). It is the Father **"...which hath made us meet** (qualified us) **to be partakers of the inheritance of the saints in light"** (Col. 1:12). Immediately following this faith is repentance. This repentance, too, is not a work of man's but is a Gift from God: **"...the goodness of God leadeth thee to repentance"** (Rom. 2:4). God **"...now commandeth all men everywhere to repent"** (Acts 17:30). Not merely a repentance of one's immorality such as adultery, stealing and drunkenness etc., but a repentance from dead works and idolatry. Works which were once considered to have endeared one to God are called fruit unto death (Rom. 7:5); and any worship of anyone or anything but the True God is called idolatry (Ex. 20:3). Man must repent of his sins. He must repent of all his idolatry and dead works. He must turn from and consider as dung (excrement, refuse) **(just as the apostle Paul did)** all his religious works and efforts, prior to believing THE Gospel, in trying to please a Holy God in order to merit salvation, to in any way contribute to his salvation, or at least to contribute to maintaining his own salvation. This man will never believe, once saved, that anything he does or abstains from doing is in any way contributing to his remaining saved. Man needs to repent of ever believing that anything he ever did or abstained from doing made him more acceptable to a Holy God. **Everything a man did and believed which he thought recommended him unto God before he heard and believed the true and only Gospel of God must be shunned and abhorred as nothing but idolatry and fruit unto death,** in order that they might win Christ and be found with HIS Righteousness and not their own; for the Bible teaches that no man will be saved according to what he has done or abstained from doing. All that the apostle Paul once thought and believed recommended him to God he instantly rejected upon hearing God's Gospel which speaks of Christ's Righteousness and not man's: **"But what things were gain to me, those I counted loss for Christ. Yea doubtless, and I count all things but loss for the excellency of the knowledge of Christ Jesus my Lord: for whom I have suffered the loss of all things, and do count them but dung, that I may win Christ, and be found in Him, NOT HAVING MINE OWN RIGHTEOUSNESS, which is of the law, but that which is THROUGH THE FAITH OF CHRIST THE RIGHTEOUSNESS WHICH IS OF GOD BY FAITH"** (Phil 3:7-9; see also Rom. 10:1-4; Gal. 2:16). This is TRUE godly Repentance which no true believer will ever deny! If any man hangs onto and relies upon anything he did or abstained from doing in his past (before belief in the Gospel), or seeks to cling to in the future to recommend him to God other than the Blood and Righteousness of Christ, **Christ shall profit him nothing.** That man does not believe the Gospel of Christ and is yet in his sins.

A true believer believes that every one of God's chosen will be saved, that not one will be lost. A true believer believes that the Holy Spirit of God comes to every chosen vessel, at the appointed time, and makes that man alive to God, spiritually regenerates him, in order that he will come to God God's Way, that he will understand and seek God according to the Scriptures: **"But there is a spirit in man: and the inspiration of the Almighty giveth them understanding"** (Job 32:8); **"And we know that the Son of God is come, and HATH GIVEN US an understanding, that we may know Him that is true..."** (1 John 5:20). **"Thy people shall be willing in the day of Thy power..."** Psa. 110:3). As was the case with Paul the apostle so it is with every child of God **"...the God of our fathers hath chosen thee, that thou shouldest know His will, and see that Just One, and shouldest hear the Voice of His mouth"** (Acts 22:14). Christ's chosen ones hear and see Him in the Holy Scriptures. The Lord has said that He will seek out His sheep until He finds them: **"...I will both search my** *sheep, and seek them out....and **WILL deliver them...**"* (Ezek. 34:11,12; see also Luke 15:4-6). The true believer believes that none of the elect could ever resist the Holy Spirit's call and therefore 'miss out' on salvation, on God's eternal predestined plan for him for God is Almighty, He does whatsoever He pleases. Jesus said: **"ALL that the Father giveth Me SHALL come to me..."** (John 6:37), no if's, but's or maybe's about it!! **"As Thou hast given Him power over all flesh, that He should give eternal life to AS MANY as Thou hast given Him** (John 17:2). **"...EVERYONE that is of the Truth heareth My voice"** (John 18:37). **"And other sheep I have, which are not of this fold: them also I MUST bring, and they SHALL hear My voice..."** (John 10:16; see also verses 4,5). No man or devil could ever thwart any plan of God's, for then God would cease to be God: **"But our God is in the heavens: He hath done whatsoever He hath pleased"** (Psa. 115:3). **"...He doeth according to His will in the army of heaven, AND among the inhabitants of the earth: and none can stay His Hand, or say unto Him, 'What doest Thou?'"** (Dan. 4:35). God says of Himself: **"...I AM God, and there is none else; I am God, and there is none like Me, declaring the end from the beginning, and from ancient times the things that are not yet done, saying, My counsel SHALL stand, and I WILL do all My pleasure... yea, I have spoken it, I WILL also bring it to pass; I have purposed it, I WILL also do it"** (Isa. 46:9-11). This should convince anyone that God does whatever He wants and whatever He wants to do He does!! **"Consider the work of God: for who can make that straight, which He hath made crooked?"** (Eccl. 7:13).

Salvation is not conditional on what a man does but on what Christ HAS DONE because of God's mercy. *"The very concept of grace is salvation conditioned on Christ."* The Bible teaches that: **"Therefore hath He mercy on whom HE WILL have mercy, and whom He will he hardeneth"** (Rom. 9:18). Salvation is conditioned on the work of Christ by the mercy of God, and according to the Holy Scriptures, to whomsoever God wills to be merciful, HE WILL be merciful! Whom He wills to be saved WILL BE SAVED!! **"Blessed is** *the man whom Thou choosest, and causest to approach unto Thee..."* (Psa. 65:4; see also John 6:44). The only way a man CAN come to God is if God has chosen him to come; therefore, all whom He has chosen WILL come for who has resisted His will? (Rom. 9:19). *"...as many as were ORDAINED to eternal life BELIEVED"* (Acts 13:48; see also Acts 22:14). Peter the apostle said *"...God made choice among us, that the Gentiles by my mouth should hear the Word of the Gospel, AND BELIEVE"* (Acts 15:7). All whom God has chosen to be objects of His mercy WILL at the appointed time believe; that is why the chosen of God are described as blessed—blessed of God. *"Of His own will begat He us with the Word of Truth* (the Gospel)*..."* (James 1:18); *"Being born again, not of corruptible seed, but of incorruptible, by the Word of God, which liveth and abideth forever...And this is the Word which by the Gospel is preached unto you"* (1 Pet.1:23,25). *"But OF HIM are ye in Christ Jesus..."* (1 Cor.1:30). Salvation is God's predetermined and eternal plan for all His people, His elect ones, and all whom He calls WILL come to Him not because they are any better or more moral or holier than others but purely because this is the will of God; not because they are righteous but because HE is Righteous and Faithful to His promise to save all for whom Christ died. They will all be made alive, born again, regenerated without fail. Not one will miss out: *"Therefore it is of faith, that it might be by grace; to the end the promise might BE SURE to ALL the seed..."* (Rom. 4:16).

Finally, not only will the true believer believe that every one whom God has chosen will be saved, he will also believe that his salvation is **eternal**—that the truly saved man can never lose his salvation. The Christian simply believes the Words of His Savior: *"My sheep hear My voice, and I know them, and they follow Me: And I give unto them ETERNAL LIFE; and they shall NEVER PERISH, neither shall any man pluck them out of My Hand. My Father, which gave them Me, is GREATER THAN ALL; and no man is able to pluck them out of My Father's Hand"* (Jn. 10:27-29; Jer. 32:40). Obviously, then, all who have been elected, forgiven, and made alive unto God WILL

NEVER fall away or perish and return to a lost state again for the life they have been given is ETERNAL! Their life is hid with Christ in God (Col. 3:3). The forgiveness of their sins—past, present and future—is an eternal forgiveness: What the law could not do Jesus Christ DID DO: **"And by Him all that believe are JUSTIFIED from ALL THINGS, from which ye could not be justified by the law of Moses"** (Acts 13:39). **"There is therefore now NO condemnation to them which are in Christ Jesus, who walk not after the flesh, but after the Spirit"** (Rom. 8:1). Unless God's Law is completely obeyed to the letter it can only condemn. God's Law has never pronounced an unrighteous man righteous. **"For what the law could not do, in that it was weak through the flesh, God sending His own Son in the likeness of sinful flesh, and for sin, condemned sin in the flesh"** (Rom. 8:3). *"What is it the law could not do? It could not pronounce any sinner justified, pardoned, saved, fit for, or entitled to salvation based on that sinner's character and conduct, not because of any weakness in the law, but because of the sinfulness of the sinner. Everything we do in our character and conduct falls short of the standard of perfect righteousness* (which the law demands). *Nothing we do measures up.* (WP). The Righteousness that has been established for God's elect and imputed to their account is an everlasting Righteousness. The word 'saved' means 'preserved'. The true believer is said to be: **"...sanctified by God the Father, and PRESERVED in Jesus Christ, and called"** (Jude 1). The psalmist says of the Lord's saints: **"...the Lord loveth judgement, and forsaketh not His saints; they are PRESERVED forever..."** (Psa. 37:28). They will always be in right standing with God not because of themselves or based on anything they do but who they are in Christ Jesus the Lord Who died for their sins and gave them His own Righteousness so that they could be with Him forever, therefore, **"Who shall lay anything to the charge of God's elect? It is God that justifieth"** (Rom. 8:33). The Scripture tells us that after we believed **"...ye were sealed** (preserved) **with that Holy Spirit of promise, which is the earnest** (guarantee) **of our inheritance until the redemption of the purchased possession, unto the** *praise of His glory"* (Eph. 1:13,14). John the apostle said: **"We know that we HAVE PASSED from death unto life..."** (1 John 3:14).

Since the believer born of God will believe that salvation from God is not dependant on what a man does—since he believes that he can do nothing to gain, merit, or maintain salvation in any way—he believes that he can never do anything to lose that salvation, for Christ Jesus has paid the price of that man's EVERY SIN forever, including the only unforgivable sin, the sin of unbelief; the sin that damns every man by nature and which NO true believer can ever commit for he has been made eternally alive unto God who has delivered them **"...from the power of darkness, and hath translated us into the Kingdom of His dear Son"** (Col. 1:13), and that eternally. A saved man can never again fall back into the sin of unbelief for he has been made to believe forever. Christ Jesus the Lord has obtained for him **eternal** redemption and has given him His Own Righteousness, **"...by His own blood He entered in once into the Holy Place, HAVING OBTAINED ETERNAL REDEMPTION for us"** (Heb. 9:12). God's people have been bought back (redeemed) not temporarily but forever!!. **Salvation is not a temporal blessing but an ETERNAL one.** If God is the Author of your faith you **will** believe to the end for His faith **preserves. "Being confident of this very thing, that He which hath begun a good work in you WILL perform it until the day of Jesus Christ"** (Phil. 1:6; see also Psa. 138:8; 1 Thess.5:23,24). **One cannot lose what Christ has earned.** The Faith that comes from God gives a man the certain assurance that he is saved and will remain saved based on what Christ has done. Those who believe one can lose their salvation show they are either ignorant of or have no confidence in the salvation that is conditional on Christ alone. **Oh, the prideful arrogance of sinful man to ever think that he could do anything to get saved or stay saved.** They have yet to believe God's ONLY Gospel. In contrast, the true believer places no confidence in himself (Rom. 7:18; Phil. 3:3). The apostle Paul assures us that the true Christian is not among those **"...who draw back unto perdition; but of them that believe to the saving of the** *soul"* (Heb. 10:39). Those who do *draw back* are said to HAVE NEVER BEEN TRUE BELIEVERS: **"They went out from us, but they were not of us; for if they had been of us, they would NO DOUBT HAVE CONTINUED with us..."** (1 John 2:19). The Bible teaches that the Lord Jesus **"...shall also CONFIRM YOU UNTO THE END, that ye may be blameless in the day of our Lord Jesus Christ"** (1 Cor.1:8). The saved sinner has been made alive to God ETERNALLY. **"For by one offering He hath perfected FOREVER them that are sanctified"** (Heb. 10:14)., therefore God says: **"...I will never leave thee, nor forsake thee"** (Heb. 13:5). The life which the believer has been given is an everlasting life which cannot be lost, for, the blood that Christ shed for His people, that has washed away their sins, is **"...the blood of the EVERLASTING covenant"** (Heb. 13:20), a covenant incidentally which was made between the Father and the Son, which neither can break (that is why it is everlasting), and which all true believers have been brought into purely by Grace alone. Man is **saved** by the Power of God and he is also **kept** by the Power of God. The apostle Peter stated that the saved man has been begotten **"...to an inheritance INCORRUPTIBLE, and UNDEFILED, and that FADETH NOT AWAY, RESERVED in heaven for you, who are KEPT by the power of God..."** (1 Pet. 1:4,5). The Bible states that by means of Christ's death **"...they which are called might receive the promise of ETERNAL inheritance"** (Heb. 9:15). God's work cannot be undone. What He does is eternal: **"I know that, whatsoever God doeth, it shall be for ever: nothing can be put to it, nor anything taken from it: and God doeth it, that men should fear before Him"** (Eccl. 3:14).

Every false gospel out there, every false religion—and the deadliest are those which come in the name of Christ Himself—teaches that salvation is conditioned on what a man does. Man must do this or that, he must lead a life of abstinence, of separation, of holiness, of sabbath keeping or of prayer or of good works and of church attendance, of strict obedience to God's law if he is to have any chance of pleasing God and ultimately reaching heaven. This is what every man believes by nature. This is the sin that deceives all men by nature. In essence, they all teach that man must establish his own righteousness in order to please God—that Christ's Righteousness alone is not enough. They do not believe in salvation by grace ALONE. Every religious person out there believes he must and can do something to please God in order to be saved. The Jews sought after righteousness with God but they did not attain to it: *"Wherefore? Because they sought it not by faith, but as it were by the works of the law..."* (Rom. 9:32). The apostle Paul added: *"For they being ignorant of God's Righteousness, and going about to establish their own righteousness, have not submitted themselves unto the Righteousness of God"* (Rom. 10:3). In contrast, the true believer waits, through the Spirit, *"...for the hope of righteousness BY FAITH"* (Gal. 5:5). False gospels and false religions—including those which come in Christ's name—do not teach that salvation is in one Man Jesus Christ **ALONE**, but that man must obey the law of God and/or various traditions of men in addition to what Christ has done in order to one day secure salvation or at least maintain it. They do not promote the teaching that Jesus' Blood and Righteousness is enough for a sinner to be made right with God and to remain in right standing with God and to hope in nothing less; instead, they always add that man must contribute his part. Paul the apostle taught that if a man were to add even a small thing such as circumcision to his salvation then it is a false gospel he trusts in and Christ would not profit that man AT ALL: *"...I Paul say unto you, that if ye be circumcised, Christ shall profit you nothing"* (see Gal. 5:1-3). If you believe that you can do anything to get saved then Paul says that you are *"...a debtor to do the whole law"* (Gal. 5:3) for that's what it will take to get any man into heaven. The WHOLE Law of God must be fulfilled not part of it. Either you believe Righteousness can be achieved by your obedience to the law or through Christ ALONE Who HAS obeyed it. Any system of works which is adhered to—even believing that faith was a condition for salvation which YOU fulfilled and praise God for—which a man believes is necessary to his salvation in addition to Christ's work of Redemption will damn him eternally. Make the minutest addition to Christ's Gospel, attribute any part of salvation to man, and you have another gospel, a gospel that is not of grace but of works, wherein there is NO salvation: **"A little leaven leaveneth the whole lump"** Gal. 5:9). **You MUST believe CHRIST'S GOSPEL and reject all counterfeits.** A godly man has wisely stated: *"God's Gospel reveals Christ's Righteousness that entitles sinners to all of salvation, and it exposes the sin that deceives us all by nature, the sin of thinking that anything could recommend us unto God or entitle us to heaven but the Righteousness of Christ ALONE.* **"For I am not ashamed of the Gospel of Christ: for IT IS THE POWER OF GOD UNTO SALVATION to every one that believeth...For THEREIN is the Righteousness of God revealed..."** (Rom. 1:16,17). Righteousness is not found in our faith in the Gospel but in Christ alone as revealed in the Gospel.

Many teach a 'christ'; they even call him *'Jesus'*; but it is not THE Jesus Christ of the Bible. Their 'christ' did not do enough to secure anyone's salvation, they always teach *christ plus YOU* in one form or another. *'Salvation is by grace,'* they say, *'BUT we must also do our part to maintain salvation, by believing and then maintaining a life of good works and as few sins as possible.'* They do not believe that salvation is by grace ALONE and by the merits of Christ ALONE. Many believe that it is their work of faith which makes them righteous and recommends them to the Holy God. **They never realise that faith is a Gift from God, not a work of man's,** which points one to Christ and His Righteousness imputed to the sinner which makes the sinner Righteous. They never tell you that salvation is by grace **ALONE**, and by Christ **ALONE**, through the GIFT OF FAITH **ALONE.** Their *'reasoning'* shows that they do not believe that Christ's work ALONE makes the difference between heaven and hell but whether the sinner chooses Him or rejects Him. It is really not Christ that saves but their faith which 'saves' them; it is their faith in God they have put their trust in. Their 'gospel' is a subtle system of works which teaches that a man must believe to get saved rather than the Scriptural doctrine that a man is saved by God's grace and **therefore** believes because he has received the Gift of Faith something which he could not produce. The blind man is not healed because he can see, but he can see because he is healed. A newborn baby is not alive because it breathes, but it breathes because it is alive. So, too, the believer believes because he has been made alive by God. The Bible asks: **"For who maketh thee to differ from another? and what hast thou that thou didst not receive?..."** (1 Cor.4:7). Most people believe that it is their faith that makes them to differ from the lost but the true believer knows that it is Christ ALONE that makes him to differ from those who do not believe. The apostle Paul said: **"But by the grace of God I am what I am..."** (1 Cor.15:10) and not by his faith in God.

We have established from God's own Word that man can never please God in and of himself, for man is a corrupt creature, a sinful creature whose best efforts at pleasing God fall far short of the demands of God's Holy Law and gain nothing but the wrath and judgement of God. Man's 'good' works are not evil in and of themselves but they become so when performed in an effort to make one acceptable before God. It is a rejection of Christ and what He has done to make the sinner Righteous. No matter what a child of wrath does he remains a child of wrath, **"Knowing that a man is not justified by the works of the law, but by the faith of Jesus Christ, even we have believed in Jesus Christ, that we might be justified by the faith of Christ, and not by the works of the law: for by the works of the law shall no flesh be justified"** (Gal. 2:16). This verse of Scripture shows that whatever a man does he remains in an unjustified state. The law can do nothing but demand eternal punishment for the sinner who tries to obey it in order to satisfy its demands. Man is in need of a Savior; that is why Christ came to this earth—to save sinners!! For they could never save themselves. While God's elect were still sinners Christ died on the cross for them (Rom. 5:8). The Bible teaches that Jesus shall **"...save HIS people from THEIR sins"** (Matt. 1:21). **"And by Him all that believe are justified from all things, from which ye could not be justified by the law of Moses"** (Acts 13:39). Jesus said: **"...I am the Way, the Truth, and the Life: no man** *cometh unto the Father, but by Me"* (John 14:6; see also Heb. 7:25). You cannot come to God by obeying the law *"...for by the law is the knowledge of sin"* (Rom. 3:20). The Law was given to point man to Christ: *"Wherefore the law was our schoolmaster to bring us unto Christ, that we might be justified by FAITH"* (not works) (Gal. 3:24). Jesus said HE is THE ONLY WAY to the Father not good works or religious devotion or a reformed character or sincerity of belief, not even one's faith in Christ. The way to the Father is not by works; by anything we do, have done, stopped doing, don't do, could do, should do or shouldn't do. **The Way to the Father is Jesus Christ: Who He is and what He has done.** And the only place you will find Christ Jesus the Lord is in THE Gospel—God's ONLY Gospel!!

Christianity is NOT about believing the right things in order to GET saved. Christians believe the right things, the true things, the doctrine of Jesus Christ the Lord, because they ARE saved—because they have been blessed of God and regenerated by God's Holy Spirit and made alive unto His glorious Truth. *"But we are bound to give thanks alway to God for you, brethren beloved of the Lord, because God hath from the beginning chosen you to salvation through sanctification of the Spirit AND BELIEF OF THE TRUTH: Whereunto He called you by our GOSPEL..."* (2 Thess. 2:13,14). The true evidence which shows whether a man is born again is that he believes THIS Gospel and has repented of ever believing and trusting in any other gospel, from dead works and idolatry. See how the Scriptures speak: Acts 2:42; Rom. 6:17; 16:17; 1 Tim. 1:3; 6:3.

The true believer will abide in the doctrine of Christ which has been detailed in this booklet and therefore will seek to lead a life of obedience, not that he might in some way contribute to his salvation or maintain it in any way (for salvation is an unmeritable gift of God; it is not something man can reach by his works), but as the result of his being saved by God's grace. *"For we are HIS workmanship, created in Christ Jesus UNTO* (not because of) *good works, which God hath before ordained that we should walk in them"* (Eph. 2:10). The true believer does not obey in order to become righteous; he obeys because he is righteous not in his own character and conduct but righteous in Christ: *"...in the Lord have I righteousness..."* (Isa. 45:24). The true believer has been clothed in the Righteousness of Christ: *"I will greatly rejoice in the Lord, my soul shall be joyful in my God; for He hath clothed me with the garments of salvation, He hath covered me with the robe of Righteousness..."* (Isa. 61:10). It is through obedience that we can show to God our love for Him and appreciation for what He has done for His own. The Christian will not continue in sin for *"...How shall we, that are dead to sin, live any longer therein?"* (Rom. 6:2) and *"For God hath not called us unto uncleanness, but unto holiness"* (1 Thess. 4:7). The true believer is now a new creature and is free to—and desires to—serve God God's Way, not in order to gain or maintain salvation, but as a direct result of that salvation, that which Christ has gained for him (2 Thess. 2:14). Christians, Christ's brethren, follow their Lord and live according to his Word and ways (see Rom. 6:1,2; 8:29); they will be zealous of good works (Titus 2:14). *"Therefore if any man be in Christ, he is a new creature: old things are passed away; behold, all things are become new"* (2 Cor. 5:17). This is God's Good News. His Gospel message unto His elect. Who are the elect? **All who believe THIS Gospel show they have been born again, elect and blessed of God and made alive unto Him.**

Every true child of God will believe all of the above, for this is the Gospel which God's Gift of Faith leads every chosen person to believe. This is how we can recognize a true Christian from a false christian, for all true Christians believe the same Gospel; they have the same mind: the Mind of Christ (1 John 4:6). **NO MAN IS SAVED WHO DOES NOT BELIEVE THIS GOSPEL; NO MAN IS SAVED WHO BELIEVES THAT ANYONE IS SAVED BELIEVING IN ANY OTHER GOSPEL; AND NO MAN IS SAVED WHO BELIEVES THAT HE OR ANYONE ELSE WAS SAVED BEFORE THEY HEARD AND BELIEVED THIS GOSPEL.** No one ever arrived at their destination before they actually got there! So, too, no one was ever saved BEFORE they heard and believed THE Gospel of Jesus

Christ. **"But though we, or an angel from heaven, preach any other gospel unto you than that which we have preached unto you, LET HIM BE ACCURSED"** (Gal. 1:8). Isaiah puts it this way: **"To the law and to the testimony: if they speak not according to this word, IT IS BECAUSE THERE IS NO LIGHT IN THEM"** (Isa. 8:20).

The Gospel of Jesus Christ is just that: It is HIS Gospel, HIS Good News. Its about HIM and the glorious love, grace and mercy He has shown. It is not about what man has to do to 'get saved'; it is about what Christ has done TO SAVE!!

"Are you willing to put your whole life, your efforts, beliefs, experiences, thoughts, your ties to friends and family on the line by exposing them to the Light of God's Gospel? If not, you are not really seeking God nor His way of eternal life in Christ. You are seeking confirmation of what you already believe. But when God sends His Spirit to enlighten your minds and convince us of what HE knows to be true, our whole life up to that point must be re-evaluated in light of Christ and His Righteousness. Then you will say: **'But God forbid that I should glory, save in the cross of our Lord Jesus Christ, by whom the world is crucified unto me, and I unto the world'** *(Gal. 6:14)*" (WP).

Paul the apostle had more religion than anyone of us before he believed THE Gospel, yet he did not stubbornly cling to and hope in anything he was or did or abstained from doing prior to his coming to a saving knowledge of Christ: **"But what things were gain to me, those I counted loss for Christ. Yea doubtless, and I count all things but loss for the excellency of the knowledge of Christ Jesus my Lord: for Whom I have suffered the loss of all things, and do count them but dung, that I may win Christ, and be found in Him, not having mine own righteousness, which is of the law, but that which is through the faith of Christ, the Righteousness which is of God by faith"** (Phil: 3:7-9). In his sinful nature and self-righteous condition Paul believed that his religion was bringing him closer to God, making him more and more acceptable to God when in fact his 'good works' were leading him further and further from God for in doing them he was trying to establish a righteousness of his own showing that he was ignorant of and not submitted to the only righteousness that can make a man just before God—the Righteousness of Christ!

"DO YOU HAVE A RIGHTEOUSNESS THAT ANSWERS THE DEMANDS OF GOD'S HOLY LAW AND JUSTICE? It is impossible for any sinner to have it based on character and conduct. If anyone has it, it is only by imputation, God freely giving it. We then receive it by faith" (WP).

The Scriptures speak plainly for all to understand: **"Whosoever transgresseth, and abideth not in the doctrine of Christ, HATH NOT GOD. He that abideth in the doctrine of Christ, HE HATH BOTH THE FATHER AND THE SON"** (2 John 9). To those who do not receive the True Christ of God's ONLY Gospel, Jesus Christ says: **"And ye have not this Word abiding in you: for Whom He hath sent, Him ye believe not....ye have not the love of God in you. I am come in My Father's name and ye receive Me not..."** (John 5:38, 42,43). **"If any man love not THE Lord Jesus Christ, let him be anathema** (accursed)" 1 Cor.16:22).

"If there come ANY unto you, and bring not THIS DOCTRINE, receiveth him not into your house, neither bid him God speed: For he that biddeth him God speed is partaker of his evil deeds" (2 John 10, 11).

Please Contact:

morenodalbello@yahoo.com.au

Please Visit:

www.godsonlygospel.com

Made in the USA
Monee, IL
03 May 2026

49437978R00022